Lucien Bély

Wonderful
Mont Saint-Michel

Translated by
Angela Moyon

Top: *The Mont seen from the west.*
Middle: *The Guest's Room.*
Bottom: *The Mont at night.*

Right: *Aerial view of the Mont.*

Back cover: *Aerial view of the abbe*
(top): *the cloisters* (bottom).

The story of the rock, the forest and the sea

Try to imagine the Mont Saint-Michel before anything was built on it. It was a two hundred and fifty foot high rock with sheer sides. The granite which it is made up of, a very hard rock which, for thousands of years, has resisted erosion from wind and water. This is the reason why this rock, together with one or two others, stands out in what is generally low-lying country.

Around the rock there was a thick forest, which may have been called Scissy Forest. It has now disappeared, for the sea over the years engulfed it. Some tree trunks have actually been found buried in the sand. According to legend, an enormous tidal wave swept over the area, transforming it completely at the beginning of the 8th century when Bishop Aubert dedicated the rock to Saint Michael. Ever since then, it has been an island just like the rock next to it, which is known as Tombelaine.

The tide in the bay where the rock stands, is among the strongest in the world. The difference in depth of water between low and high tide in the same place is around forty feet. The beaches are almost completely flat. The sea has to come in many miles in just a few hours before reaching high water mark. The sea comes in at an amazing speed. It can be as fast as a horse at the gallop, and can prove quite dangerous for people fishing or walking on the beach.

Three rivers flow out onto the shore : the Sée, the Sélune and the Couesnon. The latter marks the boundary between Brittany and Normandy, for as the old saying goes : "The Couesnon's act of folly left the Mont in Normandy". The grey silt, known locally as "tangue", gives delicate colouring to the landscape. Grass grows on those areas of the sandy shore which are no longer covered at high tide. The sheep that graze there, are known locally as "prés-salés" (salt-meadow) sheep because of the salty tang in the grass.

In this land of sand, sky and sea was built an abbey in the style of a citadel, the overall height of which, including the church's steeple, is well over five hundred feet.

The hermits

As the Roman Empire declined, a new religion appeared : Christianity. Men who believed in one God and in his son, Jesus of Nazareth, were overrunning Europe. They swept aside Roman gods and the ancient gods who inhabited woods and pools of water. To escape from the company of their fellow men and from worldly pleasures, holy men, called hermits, lived in great poverty in lonely forests and deserted islands. The place which we now call Mont Saint-

The Mont seen from the south.

The « salt-marsh sheep » with the Mont in the background.

Michel was known in those days as Mont Tombe which meant literally "tomb on a hill". The rock no doubt attracted hermits, for Christians, perhaps from Ireland, had settled very early on around the bay and near Dol-de-Bretagne. A remarkable legend tells us how fishermen provided food for the hermits living on the Mont. Whenever a hermit went hungry, he lit a fire ; the villagers saw the smoke and loaded up a donkey with provisions. God then guided it through what remained of the Forest of Scissy until it arrived safely at the holy man's refuge. One day a wolf devoured the innocent donkey and, as a punishment, God forced it to carry all the provisions from then on.

Meanwhile, the cult of Saint Michael was spreading from the East towards Gaul. Heavenly beings were associated with Christ. Among them were the angels and the archangels Michael, Raphael and Gabriel. According to the Bible, when Lucifer, the fallen angel, compared himself with God, another angel stood up before him and shouted "Who is like God ?", in other words Mi-ka-el, or Michael. God entrusted him to lead his army, for Michael is "Prince of the Heavenly Host". He wears a suit of armour or a long white tunic. He holds a sparkling sword or lance. In the *Apocalypse,* a book written by the Apostle, Saint John, a dragon with seven crowned heads and ten horns, and a tail that swept aside the stars, threatened the Virgin Mary and her Holy Child who had just been born. Michael and his angels fought this serpent from Satan and destroyed it.

Aubert dedicates the rock to Saint Michael

The Archangel often appeared in Italy : in Rome near the castle which still bears the name Holy Angel, and at Monte Gargano, a rocky peninsular on the Adriatic Sea.

The town of Avranches, which is very close to the Mont, in the year 708 was ruled by a bishop called

A backlit aerial view.

Aubert. One night, he saw Saint Michael in a dream. The Archangel ordered him to make the rock that had just been surrounded by the sea, into a place of worship dedicated to him. Aubert did nothing about it, thinking his imagination had got the better of him. Saint Michael grew impatient with him, and when he appeared the third time, he poked a hole in Aubert's skull to make him believe. He caused many more miracles to take place, so as to convince the bishop and his followers. A bull that had been stolen, was found at the very top of the Mont, as

Michael had predicted. One story has it that Aubert was to build his church as large as the area trodden on by the bull ; according to another story, it was to occupy the space left dry in the midst of the morning dew.

Aubert fulfilled Michael's wishes and despatched messengers to Monte Gargano in Italy. They brought back some sacred relics : a piece of the red cloak worn by the Archangel during one of his apparitions, and a fragment of the altar where he had placed his foot.

When they returned, Aubert

began to construct the sanctuary. The builders received some divine assistance with their task. An old man who lived nearby was called by God to move a huge stone. Another story tells of how a small child simply touched it with his foot and pushed it over the edge. There was no drinking water on the rock, but miraculously a spring was discovered. This is now called Saint Aubert's spring.

As time went by, the rock began to be known as Mont Saint-Michel, and Aubert sent a few men to live there and pray to God and his Archangel.

The foundation of the abbey

The peace and prosperity brought by Charlemagne lasted a short while. Men from the North, or Normans, came and pillaged the coast every year. Their fast, slender boats, known as drakkars, brought widespread terror. Above all else, they pillaged sanctuaries where there were objects of gold for the glory of God. The Mont had its fair share of these dreadful expeditions. In the end, the Normans came and settled, and the king of the Franks recognised one of their chiefs, Rolf le Marcheur, or Rollon, as the "Duke of Normandy". In exchange, the formidable warrior became a Christian along with all his soldiers, and from then on protected all those in God's service.

Rollon and his descendants encouraged the rebuilding of important sanctuaries. But these new converts to the faith had high standards. Duke Richard reproached the priests who lived on the Mont for their immoral and impious behaviour. He threw them out and replaced them in 966 with submissive and humble monks from Flanders guided by a man of noble family called Maynard. These eleven monks adopted the rule of Saint Benedict which required them to organise their lives according to the principles of poverty, chastity and obedience. The abbey had become a Benedictine abbey.

The monk's leader was the abbot, or "father" of the community. He administered all the possessions of the monastery, encouraged the cult of Saint Michael, and received visitors. Theoretically, the monks themselves elected their own superior, but in practice, the Duke of Normandy, as protector of the abbey, persisted in selecting his own candidate for a long time.

The romanesque age

The monks' vocation was to pray, both for themselves and for all men. Behind the high walls of the monastery, in the "enclosure", they avoided, as far as they could, all worldly temptations and violence. Their day was divided into eight hours : Matins at daybreak, Lauds, Prime, Terce, Sext around midday, Nones, Vespers, and Compline at the end of the day. Each of these

Bottom and overleaf: An aerial view of the abbey.

THE KING'S GATE
(Porte du Roy)

One of the major preoccupations of men in the Middle Ages was fortifying the entrance to their town. Three huge gates were built to provide increased resistance to attack. The ultimate means of defence was the King's Gate protected on the south side by the two great Arcade and King's Towers. A moat, draw bridge and portcullis made it difficult to penetrate in case of attack. The coats-of-arms of the abbey, the town and the monarch, the symbols of the three levels of authority, were all added to it. The guards kept watch from the top of the parapet walk and were billetted in the King's Lodging. Leading up to this particular gate was the Boulevard and its gate, which were also designed in the 15th Century and which were defended by a redoubt and a semicircular outwork. In the 16th Century, the king's lieutenant completed the defensive system by building the Forward Gate (Porte de l'Avancée). The « bourgeoisie » i.e. the town's inhabitants, had to take turns to keep watch from this gate and to each side is the Bourgeois' Guardroom. Battlements overlooked the courtyard containing the bombards captured from the English.

THE NORTH-EAST CORNER OF THE ABBEY: THE MARVEL AND THE BARBICAN

There is no doubt about it; the abbey is a citadel. Although the steep sides of the rock made attack difficult, men throughout the ages have tried their best to protect the monastery. The Romanesque buildings already had a good system of defence. The Gothic Marvel, with its three storeys, its proud walls, and its mighty buttresses, appears to be impregnable. With the first rumours of war came the continuation of military effort and in the late 14th Century Pierre le Roi had the barbican built. After the long siege of the Mont by the English, Captain Louis d'Estouteville designed a first-class system of defense. All the ramparts were strengthened between 1425 and 1440, and the entire town was surrounded by a wall. As improvements had been made to firearms during various conflicts, the design allowed for their use here — they were, after all, an active means of defence.

hours was accompanied by prayers which were read out of "books of hours", or breviaries.

Knights, in feudal times, engaged themselves in the profession of arms. But as death grew near, they turned to the abbeys. A captain, Néel de Saint-Sauveur, sought refuge and peace on the Mont Saint-Michel. Many warriors too asked to be buried in holy ground near sanctuaries.

When the old buildings were no longer big enough, the abbey, because of its wealth, was able to expand. An immense church was built at the top of the rock, to serve as a grandiose setting for prayer. Building techniques had progressed in Normandy. The style of architecture that later came to be known as Romanesque, was at its height. With the help of strong supporting pillars and huge arches to support beams and domes, the walls could be built extremely high. Two high towers, now no longer there, used to set off the façade of the church. To support this church, crypts, or subterranean chapels, were built along the contours of the rock. Their vaults, such as the one in the Saint-Martin crypt, were works of art. The very weight of the stones and the ingenious stonework ensured that the building was sound. The monks liked to pray in the half-light of the crypts. The living quarters, known as the "convenuels", occupied three floors in the northern part of the abbey. The dormitory (now the sacristy) was near the church ; below was the monks' promenade that has often been transformed over the ages ; finally, near the north-west door, was the so-called Aquilon room, built in the Romanesque style, where pilgrims were received.

Famous pilgrims

Very soon, famous pilgrims came to the Mont Saint-Michel to implore the Archangel's protection. Richard II, Duke of Normandy,

(continued on page 19)

THE ABBEY LODGINGS
The abbot lived here, close to the pilgrims, while the monks sought peace in the « enclosure » on the north side. This, then, is the « worldly » part of the abbey built gradually from the 13th to the 16th *Centuries. The accommodation was sometimes known as the « Abbot's Palace ». Those chiefly responsible for its existence were Pierre le Roi (1386-1419) and Guillaume de Lamps (1499-1510).*

An aerial view of the Mont.

THE WEST FRONT OF THE CHURCH AND ITS ORIGINAL LAYOUT

From the 16th to the 19th Centuries, the buildings fell into disrepair. The Benedictines of the Maurist Rule, who were great philosophers but poor builders and inadequate artists, tried to live in the ruins of the monastery. The first three spans of the church were demolished in the late 18th Century. The Classical façade was completed in 1780. Its austerity and unobtrusiveness is particularly suitable for the Mont. Golden-yellow lichen adds a touch of colour to the bare stone. The Romanesque façade was also very plain. It was flanked by two towers that were reminiscent of the ones in Jumièges and which had been built by Robert de Thorigny. One of them was demolished in the late Middle Ages; the other one on the south side, the Clock Tower, survived until the fire in 1776. The first spans were replaced by this west-facing platform, called the « Plomb du Four », the « layout of the end of the nave ». It looks westward towards the Isles Chausey which provided the granite used on the Mont. The present sacristy on the left of the West Front is in fact the former dorter, the upper storey of the Romanesque monastery buildings. The short distance separating it from the church enabled the monks to go to the sanctuary in the dark to hear Matins.

Left:

THE GREAT INNER STAIRCASE

In the Middle Ages, «entry» into a town or an abbey involved grandiose ceremonies when the visitor was powerful and famous. It was a sacred act which was finally subject to rules laid down by tradition. The king was received at the town gates, the Archibishop of Rouen at the top of the town, and the Bishop of Avranches at the entrance to the abbey. The entrance ceremony was a reflection of social hierarchy. The architecture, then, had to provide a majestic backdrop to the slow climb up the rock. The Staircase, with its landings and wide steps, was an integral part of the ceremonial. In order to give it its real importance, successive abbots had no hesitation in altering buildings further down the Mont.

The staircase runs alongside the abbey lodgings, from the bailiff's residence to the Chapel of Saint-Catherine-of-the-Staircase and the Priors' lodgings. This was the «worldly» section of the abbey and was in permanent contact with visitors.

The staircase also had a defensive rôle to fill. To reach the church, attackers would have to pass through here, through what was in fact a ditch between two high walls. Monks or soldiers could defend it from the two fortified bridges connecting the lodgings to the depths of the church.

THE NORTH WALL OF THE ROMANESQUE NAVE (12th CENTURY)

The nave in Mont Saint-Michel minster shows the progress made in architecture during the Romanesque Period. Thenceforth, the solidity of the building was based on a framework of pillars and arches rather than on a huge pile of stone. Weight and thrust were taken into consideration. « The entire building then becomes an active organism, not a passive force. A piece of masonry becomes a piece of architecture » (Germain Bazin).*

The slenderness, elegance and regularity were not achieved without disasters. One morning in 1103, while the monks were at prayer, the north wall of the nave collapsed onto the monastery buildings. It had to be rebuilt, thicker and with fewer openings. The south section of the nave, then, dates from the 11th Century while the north wall is 12th Century.

In each span, three storeys are marked out by horizontal banding — the great arches, the blind storey above, and the clerestorey at the top which lets in the light. Each span is topped by a large relieving arch — by bearing all the weight of the rafters, it enabled the builder to raise only a thin wall between the pillars. The other unusual feature is the long engaged pillar which rises to the very top of the church and which is a veritable « inner buttress ».

14

Overleaf:

THE CLOISTERS
(EARLY 13TH CENTURY)

This was the place for a stroll, conversation, and meditation. It is the last floor of the Marvel and was reserved for the monks. The garden, halfway between the sea and the sky, is surrounded by covered walkways. It lies on the same level as the refectory and the church and rests on the vaulting in the

Knights' Room. In order to lay out this space, which was both open and enclosed, the north transept of the abbey church was shortened at the spot where a huge Gothic window was built. The side walls were made of granite. In the south gallery (on the right), relieving arches with fine springing support the gable end of the transept. The lavatorium or lavabo was laid out with a double bench and a fountain, all at ground level. The abbot would celebrate the ceremony of the Washing of

the Feet here, in memory of Christ. The monks would wash there before meals. The west gallery (on the left) was to open onto the chapter house but it was never built. The three bay windows were to have been the doorways. In the corner of the galleries, two narrow quirks leave bare a limestone colonette above the one made of fine-grained granite. In the Middle Ages, the walkways were covered with slats of wood known as the « essentes ». A grey schist roof has since replaced them.

Right:

THE FLAMBOYANT GOTHIC CHANCEL
(1450-1521)

Its design was based on the nave in Rouen's Saint-Ouen, the abbey for which Guillaume d'Estouteville was also Abbot. The original plans may have been drawn by the same architect in both cases, Guillaume Pontis. Saint-Ouen was considered in the late Middle Ages as one of the highlights of Gothic architecture. The 15th-century project for the Mont was scrupulously adhered to, although the building work was completed by Guillaume et Jean de Lamps in the early 16th Century. Four centuries, then, separate the Romanesque nave and the chancel that may be seen as a final expression of mediaeval architecture.

Everything has been sacrificed to the sense of verticality. The pillars are devoid of capitals. The narrowness of the arches in comparison to their height emphasises the impression of an upward vertical swing. Each span is also broken up by three storeys — the arch, the triforium or blind storey, and the clerestorey.

In the chancel, Flamboyant Gothic architecture played around, albeit austerely, with solids and empty spaces. The robust architecture becomes a fragile stone skeleton towards the top of the buildings. The architect also played with light and shade. Bright daylight floods through the windows from which the Renaissance stained glass has disappeared.

(continued from page 11)

married Judith of Brittany there in the presence of the nobility of both provinces. On that occasion, he offered the abbey some churches, mills, lands and forests. One Duke of Brittany placed on the altar, property deeds of lands which he was making over to the monastery. These numerous gifts amounted to a vast amount of property all around the Bay. Peasants, that worked on these lands, regularly transported to the island, either by boat or on carts at low tide, part of their harvests. In exchange they received protection and justice.

The abbot, in his turn, honoured the protectors of the abbey. When Duke William completed the conquest of England, the superior of the Mont sent six ships and four monks to salute the new king. The finest of all the abbots was Robert de Thorigny who had been a skilful member of the Court of the Plantagenet King, Henry II, who reigned over England and a large part of France. This abbot administered the abbey at the peak of its fortune.

Left:
COLONETTES IN THE CLOISTERS
The shafts may have been carved in England and imported into France. Originally, they were probably made out of a fine-grained limestone, similar to marble. The architect Corroyer, though, preferred a fine-grained granite. The hardness of this stone explains the prismatic outline and the simplicity of the plinths, bases and abaci. The colonettes were placed in staggered lines, i.e. instead of being in pairs, they are in two rows that are slightly out of line with each other. They are connected by arches along the same two rows, and « diagonal » arches indicate small triangular vaults. This succession of tripods gives the building absolute stability since the weight and load are shared out regularly. The technique, which was quite unknown previously in cloisters, was nevertheless not rare in Norman Gothic architecture where it was frequently incorporated into doorways. As this style of architecture was not fond of empty spaces, large crochets decorated with leaves, were carved beneath the arches.

He welcomed there a whole line of magnificent princes. King Henry II, whom he served as counsellor, came and visited him, accompanied by King Louis VII of France, the Archbishop of Rouen, two cardinals who later became Popes, and five abbots. Their entrance into the abbey was an occasion for sumptuous ceremony. The entire community awaited the royal visitors on the shore at the entrance to the town with the Gospels, incense and holy water. All the bells rang out as the distinguished gathering made for the church.

Robert de Thorigny added to the community by recruiting a larger number of monks during his travels ; he enriched the library, and finally had built, on the south-west side of the abbey, a huge hostel for pilgrims, which collapsed at the beginning of the 19th century. On the west side, he built his own quarters.

A SQUINCH IN THE CLOISTERS
Between the arches in the cloisters, the soft Caen limestone has been carved. The squinches are fairly conclusive proof of the extent to which Norman architecture was fond of stone tracery. Two compositions were chosen — a rose surrounded by three other small roses, and a leaf design filling the entire triangular section. The plant theme predominates, especially the vine, because it

The miracles
Whenever some strange, fortuitous event occurred on the Mont, it was always attributed to the influence of Saint Michael. The monks built up a whole collection of these "miracles" which pilgrims and travellers passed down over the centuries.

One day, a blind woman stood in front of the Mont, and when her face turned towards it, she recovered her sight. "How beautiful it is to be able to see", she exclaimed and the name Beauvoir (beautiful to see) was given to the village where she was. Another woman, who was expecting a child, unwisely attempted to cross the shore. She suddenly felt the first birth pangs and fell to the sand. The tide was coming in, but a miracle took place and she was spared. When the fishermen found her safe and sound, her child had been born.

The men of the Middle Ages thought that the bones of saints

gave great scope for the sculptor's imagination. All the motifs are reduced to a sense of movement, to a pure interplay of line and shape. The cavity carved out in the wall provides a dark background from which the swirls of the carvings stand out. A frieze runs along the cloister walls above the squinches, showing a barn owl between two roses. The decorative features were originally painted in bright colours.

had miraculous powers. The bones of Bishop Aubert, now Saint Aubert, had disappeared. A long time after the foundation of the abbey, a piece of music, that the monks thought had been sent from heaven, began to be heard. They started to look for it and questioned the nephew of one of the canons who had previously been expelled. At last, some chests were found hidden in the dormitory ceiling. A miraculous force caused the locks to open and inside were the Saint's relics. A parchment was found, that proved the authenticity of the bones.

Religious feasts

The men of the Middle Ages liked religious feasts. The architecture of the Mont, with its huge church, mysterious crypts and great stairways, lent itself well to splendid ceremonies.

There were frequent processions through the abbey. The abbot then, just like a bishop, wore a mitre and carried a crook. The monks, instead of their severe, rough habits, wore copes (sleeveless cloaks), or white habits known as albs. The whole monastery was lit up with candles. The relics in their reliquaries, and the Gospels, were taken among the pilgrims in

(continued on page 28)

THE WHEEL, THE HOIST
(19th CENTURY),
AND THE ROMANESQUE
OSSUARY
The Romanesque abbey was extended on the south side by buildings desi-

gned to accommodate pilgrims. It was Robert de Thorigny who had the hostelry built, a large chamber with ribbed barrel vaulting and three tall windows. On the lower floor, there was to be an undercroft where the

food was stored. On the upper floor, the monks installed the infirmary that was so vital for the community and its visitors. These three storeys collapsed in 1817. The only reminder of them these days is a model kept in the Invalides Museum. The infirmary opened onto St. Stephen's Chapel, the mortuary chapel where it is thought the bodies were laid out. It had 13th-century ogival vaulting. The monks' ossuary was next to the chapel. Death, then, was an integral part of the architectural plan. The prison service installed a huge wheel in this ossuary and prisoners walked around inside it to make it turn. A trolley would then be drawn up along a hoist, a veritable stone ladder snaking its way up the wall of rock. It was, in fact, a reminder of the Middle Ages since it resembled the one used by the monks. One of them was in use for many years in the Romanesque undercroft and there was a second one in the Gothic undercroft in the Marvel. It was the latter system which was used by a captain during the Wars of Religion in his attempt to enter the citadel.

Right:

THE CRYPT
OF THE MIGHTY PILLARS
(1446-1450)

The Romanesque chancel collapsed in 1421 but war made rebuilding impossible. Once peace had been restored, Cardinal d'Estouteville, the influential abbot of the Mont, ordered the work to begin. The Crypt of the Mighty Pillars was erected in only a few years and was designed to support the new chancel. Ten enormous cylindrical columns were built, perhaps around the original Romanesque pillars. Two of them, which are smaller than the rest, were given the descriptive name «palm trees».

ST.MARTIN'S CHAPEL

The St.Martin Crypt bears the weight of the south transept of the abbey church. Its semicircular barrel vault is a model of rigourous austerity. It is reinforced in the centre by a ribbed arch. At the east end is an apsidal chapel with one window supporting the apsidal chapel in the upper church.

The stone arch was the major feature from the Middle Ages. The dim atmosphere was particularly well-suited to the funeral rites to which the abbey devoted itself. The noblemen of the day preferred to be laid to rest in the shade of a sanctuary. The vaulting also improved the acoustics in the chapels. And after all, plainsong was the monks' only passion and perhaps even their supreme contribution to the arts. Vaulting also had two symbolic meanings according to Mr. G. Duby. By replacing the wood with stone, the Benedictines had given the building «a substantial unity which made it a more fitting representation of the universe, itself a total unity within the divine Will. Finally, and most importantly, vaulting brought the circle into the architectural rhythms, i.e. an image of circular time, a perfect infinite line, the clearest symbol of eternity, of the heaven for which the monastic church was intended to be the antechamber». (G. Duby, «Adolescence de la chrétienté occidentale»).

OUR-LADY-UNDERGROUND (MID 10th CENTURY)

This is the Preromanesque church. It was built in the middle of the 10th Century, at the time of the abbey's foundation. Its two parallel aisles are separated by a wall opened by two arches. Carolingian traditions are apparent here in several places. The Cyclopean wall at the end of the chapel may be a throwback to the former oratory dating from the 8th and 9th Centuries. The church, which originally stood in the open air, became a crypt when the Romanesque nave was built. It was badly damaged in the 18th Century then restored in the 20th. Prestressed concrete was used to bear the weight of the minster.

On the same level near the covered walk is a crypt known as the Crypt of the Thirty Candles, which provides the base for the north transept. This chapel, in which the Virgin Mary's clothes were kept, was the spiritual centre of the abbey. Its vestibule, in which the central pier is decorated with Gothic foliage, was used as a prison and was known as the « Devil's Dungeon ».

On previous page:

THE REFECTORY
(EARLY 13th CENTURY)

Monastic meals were veritable ceremonials. It took major feats of technical skill to embellish the room in which they were taken. Setting aside any question of a vaulted ceiling which would probably have been too heavy, the architects preferred to erect semi-circular rafters, a huge upturned hull built in the Gothic period but that was nevertheless reminiscent of the nave in the Romanesque part of the church. A thick wall bore this continual weight and, in order to avoid weakening it with huge bay windows, narrow windows scarcely wider than slits were built. Set deep in the walls, they are invisible from the entrance to the refectory although they provide an astonishing amount of light. Each of them is flanked by slender colonnettes. Meals were taken in silence while one of the monks read holy texts. The pulpit stands in the south wall and, thanks to the excellent acoustics, the entire chamber was filled with his voice. The cellarer's office and kitchen were on the south side of the refectory.

THE MONKS' GALLERY
(12th CENTURY)

This long chamber represents a turning point in architectural design. Roger II originally had groined arches built but Bernard du Bec had them replaced by ogival arching after the fire in 1138. Two ribs set between transverse ribs cross each other diagonally. This technique, which gives the vaulting greater fullness, is a forerunner of Gothic architecture. Two aisles separated by five pillars stand above the rock to the east and the Aquilon crypt to the west.

The capitals are decorated with plant motifs — stylised leaves and fleurs-de-lys. The decoration is sometimes straight, sometimes upside down. The corners of the capitals also have carvings of human beings putting their arms beneath their legs or, in some places, motifs in the shape of a purse. Two bay windows left light into the chamber.

What was the room originally intended to be used for? Nobody knows. Tradition has it that this was the Romanesque cloister where the monks relaxed and took a stroll, hence its name. The adjoining disfigured buildings are said to have been the refectory and the kitchen. The Maurists made them into latrines.

THE KNIGHTS' ROOM (EARLY 13th CENTURY)

The chamber owes its names to the order of chivalry of the Knights of St. Michael, instituted by Louis XI. Yet it seems that no meeting was ever held here. It was the « calefactory ». Huge fireplaces, with a mantelpiece right up to the roof, gave some protection against the cold. Tapestries divided the chamber off into small rooms. They also hid the raised passageway to the south along which guests went on their way to the church without disturbing the monks. The chamber was also the « great work room », the scriptorium, a quite different place to the ordinary calefactory in Benedictine monasteries. It was here that the monks copied and illuminated manuscripts.

The originality of Norman architecture comes to the fore here. Sturdiness takes pride of place ahead of elegance, and the development in design ideas is quite obvious when this chamber is compared to the Guests' Room. Here the piers are stocky. The outline of the ogival arches is more noticeable.

The torus or major piece of moulding, is set off by two deep grooves. Lastly, the almost vertical capitals are decorated with fine carvings of foliagle.

(continued from page 20)

the midst of clouds of incense. The procession came to a halt at special places where fervent prayers were said.

These ceremonies could turn into veritable theatrical shows. Monks played the parts of characters in the New Testament to help everyone understand the sacred texts, in the style of mystery plays held in front of cathedrals. In the 12th century, a monk from the Mont, who was a poet, wrote in the vernacular which all could understand (and not in Latin which was the language of the church), some verses which told the abbey's history and the miracles which had been wrought there. It was called the *Roman du Mont Saint-Michel* (The story of the Mont Saint-Michel) and was the work of a monk who had all the qualities of a real minstrel.

These ceremonies were always accompanied by singing, the monks' one passion. The human voice enhanced prayer. This plain song, or Gregorian chant, by virtue of its austerity and simplicity, was a form of worship in itself.

Finally, the reception of a new monk involved a moving ceremony. The young man's head was partly shaved : this was called the "tonsure", and was a symbol of his ecclesiastical calling. After one year's observation, he was allowed to take his vows in front of the whole community. The abbot helped him to put on a monk's habit to the accompaniment of songs of praise, and bestowed upon him a kiss of peace. For three days, he then prayed in the church. But after that, he was judged worthy to be a monk.

The marvel

At the beginning of the 13th century, the great Anglo-Norman kingdom broke up. The King of France, Philippe-Auguste, took Normandy after a number of bloody battles. In the meantime, Mont Saint-Michel was besieged by an ally of the French King. The town and the abbey were in part destroyed by fire. In order to be pardoned and to convert the monastery to his cause, Philippe-Auguste sent a large amount of gold there, for it was necessary to rebuild

A new art form, known later as "Gothic", was beginning to gain a hold. It was the age of the cathedral. The "ogival" arch led to the construction of particularly spacious and high buildings. The abbots of the Mont and their architects concentrated on the monk's living quarters. This was how the "Merveille", or "Marvel" came to be built on the north side. It was a masterpiece of Gothic architecture. The Romanesque buildings were no longer large enough to accommodate the monks, whose numbers had increased, for they too were changing with the times and were concerned with more comfort and beauty to suit their life style.

THE LACE STAIRWAY

A staircase was built in a pier on the chevet that was thicker than the others. It leads to a walkway high above the ground connected to the roof of the chancel. It is thanks to the Flamboyant Gothic architecture that the granite of the handrail and the finialed pinnacles were traceried. Through this piece of lacework carved in stone there is a view right across the Bay of Mont Saint Michel with its sandbanks and waves.

Left:
THE AQUILON CHAMBER (12th CENTURY)

The name of an icy blast was given to the Romanesque almonry because it lay on the north side of the rock. The original entrance to the abbey being to the north-west, it was in this room that pilgrims were first met. It was not connected to the monastery buildings above it in order to prevent any disruption of the monks' solitude. The staircase leading to the monks' gallery is therefore a more recent addition.

After the fire of 1112, Abbot Roger II had the wooden roof replaced by stone vaulting in an effort to diminish the fire risk. Here the vaulting is groined (formed by the penetration of two barrel vaults within the same semicircle). Ribbed vaults separate them and come down onto the 11th-century gutter-bearing wall. The chamber is divided into two passages by three pillars. The sturdy columns rest on bases with a double torus (large round moulding) and a stone cushion. The austere capitals bear volutes or swirls. The central motif is heart-shaped.

The architects were certainly ambitious to dare to build such a high and vast building on this steep rock. Enormous buttresses were built on the outside to shore up the Marvel. But, at the same time, as the construction got higher, it had to become less and less massive, so as to forestall any possibility of collapse — a not infrequent occurrence in the history of the Mont. The almonry and the store house on the bottom floor had very thick walls and strong vaults ; on the second floor, the Guests' room and the Knights' room had columns and ogival arches to support the third floor which contained the refectory and the cloister.

The stones arrived by sea at high tide from the Chausey Islands off the Mont. Stonemasons carved the granite into the correct shape. Sometimes they decorated it. Then with the help of ropes, pulleys or hoists such as the one that can still be seen at the Mont, the materials were hoisted up the scaffolding. When everything was assembled, the wooden supporting frames were removed.

The life of the monks

From now on, the monks spent most of their time in the Marvel. Poor pilgrims were welcomed in the almonry, rich ones on the floor above, in the Guests' room. Both places were near the entrance which, like it is today, was to the east, and not to the north-west as in the Romanesque era. The community kept well out of the way on the higher floors of the Marvel, near the church.

The thick walls of the refectory were pierced with long narrow windows that let in plenty of light, and supported a fine wooden "cradle" vault. Meals took place in silence while one monk read sacred texts from a pulpit situated on the south wall. The cloister, suspended in mid-air between sea and sky, was for taking a stroll, for meditation and conversation. The arcades are supported on fine columns of purple stone. Above the columns, the soft, white limestone of Caen has been carved into flowers and leaves. These carvings are an admirable example of Norman decorative art.

Before the introduction of printing, the only way of preserving and reproducing a text was to copy it by hand. This was done by the monks, who went to great pains to decorate and beautify manuscripts. This was the art of illumination. Colours and designs were used to illuminate and illustrate individual letters. The Mont was known as the "city of books", for there were so many fine works in its library. The monks were not only interested in sacred texts and prayers, but also the works of Antiquity. The "chauffoir", or hot room, was the place where the monks conducted this meticulous work, as well as everything else. This room, that was later called the " Knights' ", room, shows only too well that the monks' main enemy was the dank cold that came from the sea and the mist. They fought against it by lighting huge fires, and using tapestries and furs for insulation.

Pilgrimages

In the Middle Ages, it was considered a duty to go on a pilgrimage. The richest or the bravest went to the Holy Land, Rome or Compostella. Others had to be content with a sanctuary that was nearer home. The Mont Saint-Michel, of

XI° SIECLE

la nef comportait à l'origine sept travées dont les trois premières ont été détruites au XVIII° siècle. Sa construction peut être située dans la seconde moitié du XI° siècle après la conquête de l'Angleterre. Ses dispositions architecturales présentent un notable progrès sur les précédentes...

THE ARMS OF THE ABBEY

This coat-of-arms surrounded by carved drapes was placed at the entrance to the church in the 18th Century, behind the new West Front. The abbey's arms were given their final form only very gradually. In the 15th Century, they bore three shells. They then became the « sprinkling of black shells bearing at their head (in a horizontal band) the fleur-de-lys of France ». The abbey became a centre of pilgrimage very early on in its existence, as is shown by the shells which were the distinguishing mark of pilgrims all along their route. The fleur-de-lys, the symbol of the French monarchy, were then added to the arms. They proclaimed the King of France as the protector of the monastery and fortress. The crozier and mitre, which were sometimes added for decoration, showed the rank of the abbot who was « mitred and cro-ziered », i.e. of equivalent rank to a bishop. Each abbot also had his own family coat-of-arms. He often had them included on the stained glass windows in the church. Guillaume d'Estouteville placed his on the outer wall of the church — the decorative stone frame can still be seen on the way up the Great Inner Staircase. Guillaume de Lamps put his coat-of-arms on a pier in the south transept although only a shield is visible from Gauthier's Leap.

course, was a great Norman centre of pilgrimage, but it also attracted pilgrims from all over France and all of western Christendom. Christians went there to pray to the Archangel for their sins to be forgiven and for all their hopes to come true. Ill people especially hoped that a miracle would give them back their health, as used to happen in the legends emanating from the Mont.

Sometimes God's calling was sudden and inexplicable : a man could set off for the Mont in the middle of shoeing a horse, leaving the job unfinished. In 1333, the entire population of a village suddenly left for the Mont, forcing their parish priest to go with them and say Mass there.

A pilgrim on his way to the Mont was called a "miquelot". Like all other pilgrims, he was recognisable by his leather sack that was carried over his right shoulder, and by his roughly hewn staff. He would also have shells, the very symbols of a pilgrimage, stitched to his clothing. A pilgrim could expect help and respect on his journey. He was given shelter for the night in special inns right the way along the roads leading to the Mont. These roads were called "the ways of Paradise".

He was threatened by many a danger, among them illness and fatigue. When he finally caught sight of the famous shape of the Mont he shouted out "Mont-joie", Mount Joy, in his great relief.

(continued on page 37)

THE CORBIES TOWER

Built at the south-east corner of the Marvel, this « Rooks' (or « Corbies ») Tower » with its slit windows enabled the monks to pass from one storey to another in the Gothic monastery buildings. It was topped by the stone pyramid-shaped roof shown here. Abbot Le Roi had the high wall built joining the barbican and the tower which thenceforth became part of the abbey's defences. On the left is the south wall of the Marvel. The narrow windows in the refectory stand above the stained glass windows of the Guests' Room.

Left:
THE WEST WALL OF THE MARVEL AND THE CHARTER-ROOM

The western part of the Marvel was built after the completion of the eastern section and comprised three storeys. At the top were the cloisters, below them was the Knights' Room with its great bay window, and right at the bottom was the undercroft which was used as a cellar. Supplies were dragged up here from the sand below by means of a great wheel. A drawbridge had been slung between two mighty buttresses providing support for the building on the north side. This wing of the abbey was reserved for the brothers and formed the background to their monastic life. It was intended to build a third group of buildings even further west to include the chapter house, where the community would hold its meetings and assemblies. In fact it was never built. A few reminders of the project are still visible on this wall, which was originally built as a temporary measure and which bears the marks of the frequent hesitations and changes of mind of the architects. The three windows in the cloisters, for example, were supposed to be the doorways leading into the new wing. At the most inaccessible spot, in the north-west corner, was the charter-room where the monastery archives were kept, proof of its wealth and its past heritage. This small airy room stands on an enormous corner buttress. Above the cloisters are the chimneys of the Marvel and the pyramidal roof of the refectory.

Right:
THE GABRIEL TOWER (1524)

It was the king's lieutenant, Gabriel Dupuy, who completed the Mont's system of defence. And indeed at the beginning of the 16th Century, the skill of the military engineer was almost at the peak of perfection. The so-called Gabriel Tower is a good example of this. All the possible angles of fire were catered for. The garrison could take action against any attack with all due speed. The cannon were set up inside the thick walls. The large bastion, reminiscent of the ones in Fougères Castle, provided defence for the Fanils stores. A chimney provided an outlet for the smoke. In the 17th Century, a windmill was built on the platform.

(continued from page 33)
Miquelots at the mont

All kinds came to the Mont : invalids, pilgrims and wrong-doers mixed together, and all languages and dialects could be heard. Everyone was full of hope. Some wanted to repeat the experience of Norgod, Bishop of Avranches, who saw a bright light come down to the rock thereby revealing the presence of Saint Michael. Others even tried to spend the night in the dark church, only to give up after one of them was slapped by the invisible hand of God.

The pilgrim took part in the religious festivals. He tried to touch the reliquaries which contained the precious relics, the most curious of which were a tiny sword and shield that the archangel is said to have used to kill a dragon, and that had been brought by some miraculous means from a far-off country. The faithful pilgrim was also expected to make offerings : King Philip the Fair gave a statue covered in gold ; the poor made do with a piece of

---

THE ROOFTOPS OF THE TOWN

Mont Saint-Michel is also the « town », the small Norman village nestling at the foot of the abbey with which it has always been closely connected. The first houses were built on the north side; later, they huddled on the south side. Pilgrims would find inns and taverns awaiting them just as today's visitors find hotels and restaurants. They bought badges of pilgrimage just as tourists buy souvenirs. A narrow street leads up to the monastery. A shortcut called the chemin des Monteux was preferred by the Mont's inhabitants, the Montois. A tiny church dedicated to St. Peter welcomes the faithful. A fine carving of the head of Christ, which was ordered by André de Laure in 1483, is now kept in the sacristy. A small cemetery watched over by a granite cross stands high above the sea close to the church. A few of the old houses have been preserved, e.g. the old 15th-century Hôtellerie de la Lycorne (Unicorn Hostelry); others have been restored like Tiphaine Raguenel's House, the lady in question being Du Guesclin's wife. Others have been built in a style that is considered to be appropriate.

wax that went towards lighting the chapels.

The town nestling at the foot of the abbey welcomed the travellers. They dined in the taverns and slept in the hostelries. But important visitors were received by the abbot in the very large and bright Guests' room. Food was prepared in the two enormous hearths that were hidden from the rest of the room by sumptuous tapestries. Lavatories were installed in the north wall. The reception room with its elegant columns was richly adorned. Beneath it, however, near the entrance to the Gothic abbey, was the simple and austere almonry where the poorest people could get food.

The abbey and the one hundred years' war

War broke out at the beginning of the 14th century between France and England, and took its toll together with the plague, which was then spreading throughout the whole of Christendom. It came to be called the "One Hundred Years' War".

After the serious French defeats at Poitiers and Crécy, King Charles V began to make a comeback with the help of his constable, Bertrand Duguesclin. This Breton knight was the captain of the Mont Saint-Michel. When he left France for Spain, he entrusted his wife, Tiphaine Raguenel, to the protection of Saint Michael the Archangel. She lived in a house built at the top of the town, undertaking good works and practising the science of astrology which she was devoted to : she could read the future of the world in the movement of the stars.

On the occasion of one of his visits to the abbey, the mad King, Charles VI, made the abbot Pierre le Roi, who was an academic of some standing, into his counsellor. He immediately began to fortify the abbey. He defended the entrance by building towers, successive courtyards, and ramparts, thereby creating a veritable fort together with its "barbican". He completed the living quarters on

THE ISLAND OF TOMBELAINE

Tombelaine means « small tomb ». Like the Mont, it is an outcrop of granite spared from erosion by the sea. Today it is deserted. Yet for many years it was a modest reflection of the great abbey that was its neighbour. A chapel and a priory had been built on it. The monks used them for retreats. A Venitian philosopher worked there. Gradually, this island too became a fortress. The English captured it during the One Hundred Years' War and from there threatened the Mont's garrison. In the 17th Century, the castle belonged to Fouquet and when the Superintendant of Finance fell into disgrace, Louis XIV had the fortifications razed to the ground. Thereafter Tombelaine, where according to legend King Arthur's fiancée Hélène, had died, disappeared from the pages of the history books.

the south side. These were reserved for the abbot and for the administrative and judiciary offices.

Normandy fell into English hands in 1415, after the French defeat at Agincourt. The province was then governed by the Duke of Bedford, the brother of the English King, who succeeded in winning over to his cause a number of leading Norman personalities. Among them was the abbot of the Mont, Robert Jolivet, Pierre le Roi's successor, who accepted to be counsellor to Bedford, and received, in exchange, all the property belonging to the monastery.

The monks refused to support their treacherous abbot. Some knights, who had been dispossessed of their lands, had sought refuge with them, and they stayed faithful to the French cause, the only defender of which was the Dauphin Charles, who was later to become Charles VII, the so-called "King of Bourges"

The Romanesque chancel at the Mont collapsed and, because of the war, it was impossible to reconstruct it. One of the Mont's captains died in combat ; the small island of Tombelaine fell into

English hands ; and, as a sinister omen of things to come, the river Couesnon changed course after an unusually high tide.

The shepherd lads and lasses

During these troubled times in the first half of the XIVth century, a strange phenomenon occurred. Despite all the dangers involved, children began to go on pilgrimage to the Mont Saint-Michel. They were called the "shepherd lads and lasses" in popular ballads and tales. A chronicle from the town of Cologne in Germany contains a description of these great child crusades : "That year, there was a great pilgrimage to the Mont Saint-Michel in Normandy, a pilgrimage that lasted about two years and which was made up of small children of eight, nine, ten and twelve years of age, that came from all the towns and villages of Germany and Belgium, and other countries too. They gathered together in large numbers, abandoning their parents, and marched along, two by two, in procession. At the head of the column were students bearing effigies of Saint Michael: Children from the same area grouped together behind their own standard, which was decorated with the coats of arms of their local gentry. These children inspired pity, for they had left their homes against the wishes of their parents and without any money for the journey. Nevertheless, they remained in good health, for all along the road they were given food and drink in sufficient quantities. When they arrived at the Mont Saint-Michel, they offered their standards to the Archangel.

The siege of the mont

The beginning of the XVth. century was a critical period for the Mont Saint-Michel.

The English decided to storm this stronghold which dared to stand up to them. A citadel that was defended both by its ramparts and by the sea was impregnable. It had to be surrounded and obliged to give itself up through famine and lack of water.

The siege began in 1424. Numerous troops took up positions around the Bay. A small wooden fort called the "bastille" was constructed at Ardevon, in front of the Mont, as a refuge in the event of an attack, and in order to keep a watch over the shore. Finally, a flotilla arrived to complete the blockade, from the sea.

Some Breton noblemen commanded an expedition from Saint-Malo and skilfully attacked the English ships and managed to dis-

Overleaf: *The Mont seen from the north.*

Illuminations on Mont Saint-Michel.

perse them. This naval victory enabled the Mont to receive provisions by sea. The siege had failed utterly and the citadel had not surrendered.

For the first time in a long while, the French were able to recover their confidence. It seemed that the Archangel himself had made this victory possible, and his cult won all the more prestige. This is why Saint Michael was among those who appeared to Joan of Arc. He told her : "I am Michael, the protector of France. Arise, and go to help the King of France". And he guided the shepherd girl from Lorraine through her great adventures.

Charles VII put a very able captain, called Louis d'Estouteville, in charge of the Mont's garrison. He set about putting an end to the squabbles, schemings, pillaging and debauchery that were now common in the abbey, and had been introduced by rough, coarse soldiers who knew no better. Because

he tightened up discipline in this way, the citadel was able to withstand the last attack by the English in 1433. A fire broke out in the town, destroying the wooden houses and damaging the ramparts. The English tried to take advantage of this by coming in large numbers with terrible war engines which succeeded in breaching the walls. For a while, they thought they had taken the town, but the garrison held on, and, in the end, the English were forced to withdraw. The shore was strewn with the dead, and the knights from the Mont retrieved two enormous cannons which were set up at the entrance to the town where they can still be seen.

The knights of Saint Michael

The King at the end of the Middle Ages, Louis XI, was an able but cruel monarch. He was very devout, and even superstitious. He loved pilgrimages, which is why he twice visited the sanctuary which

symbolised the French victory over the English.

It was this that made him think of creating the Order of the Knights of Saint Michael, with the Archangel as its first member. The Duke of Burgundy, who was a great enemy of the King, already had the Knights of the Golden Fleece. But the Knights of Saint Michael were the King's own creation and were chosen from among the finest noblemen of the kingdom. They received a necklace of golden shells on which hung a medal which depicted Michael slaying the dragon, and had written on it the motto of the Order : "Immense terror oceani" (the terror of the immense ocean).

The dignitaries wore white damask robes and a red velvet head dress. They took part in splendid ceremonies presided over by the

(continued on page 46

Right: St. Aubert's Chapel seen from the gardens.

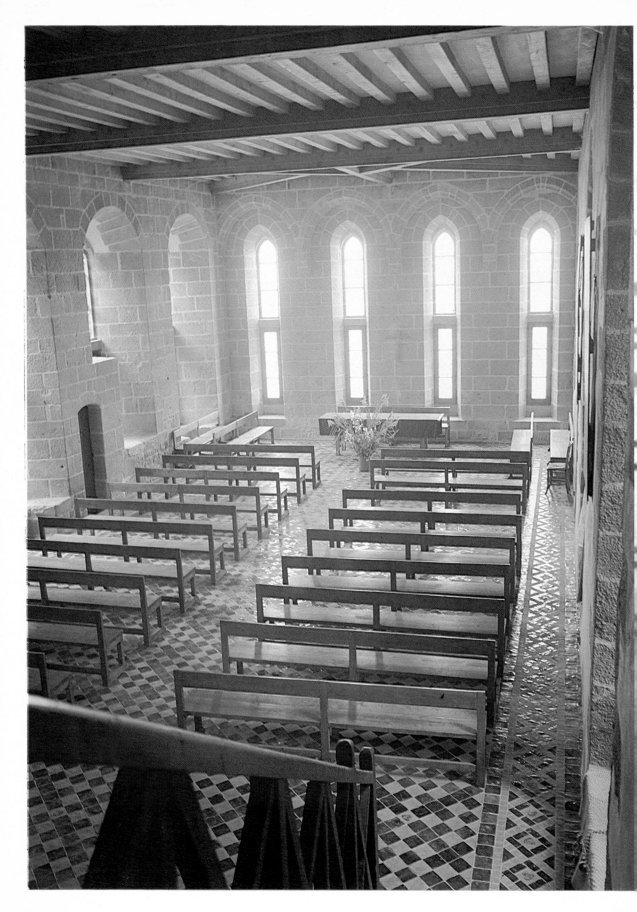

BELLE CHAISE
(MID 13th CENTURY)

Richard Turstin completed the first of the Gothic lodgings in 1257. The decadence of the 13th Century was limited. Thenceforth, the main entrance to the abbey lay to the east. On the ground floor was the gatehouse which contained the finest fireplace in the monastery, decorated with rich moulding. From 1364 onwards, visitors had to leave their weapons there. In the late 14th Century, when the Mont became a fortress, the gatehouse was made into the Guardroom. With its tall storied arches, it opens onto the great inner staircase and the abbey's lodgings, as well as onto the Gothic almonry. The room above it, with four narrow windows broken up by a transom was the seat of the abbot's court. It was there that he passed judgement, for he had the right to sentence any person on his land. The only exceptions to the rule were criminal offences, for a man of the cloth is forbidden to spill blood. He sat on a throne, the chair which gave the chamber its name. On the intervening half-floor was a small room used by the clerk of the court to complete any legal formalities. The courtroom above the gatehouse near the entrance was already a foretaste of the Romanesque abbey.

THE ENGLISH BOMBARDS

In 1434, fire raged through the town. The Montois, who had been besieged for several years, seemed to have lost all hope. The English launched an attack against the fortress. They made use of awe-inspiring weapons but were nevertheless repulsed. Large numbers of bodies lay along the shoreline and the victors carried off cannon known as «michelettes» or «miquelettes». War created its own means of destruction. The fire power of these bombards forced the inhabitants to strengthen the island's walls and reinforce the entire system of defence.

(continued from page 42)
King at the chapel of Saint Michael in the heart of Paris.

The King had another idea which was nothing short of lugubrious. He ordered a wood and metal cage to be suspended from the ceiling at the Mont. Every time the prisoner inside moved, the whole contraption began to rock. Being in this confined space in the freezing and lonely old abbey, was just like being in Hell. For centuries, political prisoners who had offended the King or his servants, were locked away there. Some were left for years at the mercy of the rats ; some ended up going mad.

The last constructions

Captain d'Estouteville had strengthened the abbey's defences. The town, which had always been threatened in war, had been encircled by ramparts and strong towers such as the Roy, Cholet, Beatrix and Arcade towers. With all its cannons, machicolations through which various objects could be dropped in defence, and watchtowers which commanded a view over the shores, the Mont Saint-Michel had become one of the strongest forts of its day. A lot of progress had been made during the long war in the art of attack and self-defence.

Abbot Jolivet had died at Rouen in the midst of the English whom he had served well. Louis d'Estouteville had appointed his brother, Guillaume, as abbot of the Mont. This man was a prince of the Church, a cardinal. He wasn't a monk but a priest. His many important commitments prevented him from devoting all his time to the monastery, which he left in the hands of the prior. Thus started the "commendam" system, which involved the abbot residing outside his community while receiving the greater part of their revenue. From that time on, the King handed over numerous abbeys to important people whom he wanted to honour or reward.

The cardinal's prestige and his influence with the Pope and the King speeded up the reconstruction of the church. A crypt, known as "the crypt of the wide pillars", supported the new construction which was finished at the beginning of the 16th century. The tall, graceful chancel is lit by high win-

The R. Couesnon, which separates Brittany on the right from Normandy on the left.

ows, and a gallery with delicate arvings and tracery. To support he building at the top of the rock, lying buttresses were positioned to ct as props. The outside was nished off with "pinnacles", or ne pyramids decorated with flo- ers. Because of its rich profusion of detail, this style was known as the "flamboyant" style. A "lace-work stairway" (the name is well chosen) gives access through this forest of granite right up to the roof, from where the whole sweep of the Bay can be seen.

The outline of the Mont seen from the hill at Avranches with Tombelaine in the background.

Overleaf:
HE GUESTS' ROOM
EARLY 13th CENTURY)

uilt by Abbot Raoul des Isles, this hamber was built for rich or famous isitors who took their meals there ith the abbot. Two aisles in which he tables were set out, two huge fire- laces where the meals were prepared nd which were separated from the

rest of the chamber by tapestries, and latrines in the north wall — these were the necessary « mod. cons. » in any reception room of the day. The elegance of the ogival arches and pil- lars, the light flooding in through the great east-facing bay windows, the beauty of the stylised foliage, and the other decorative features that have since disappeared (paintings, tiling, stained glass, and tapestries) all made Gothic architecture into a

means of displaying great pomp. Thanks to the style that originated in the Paris Basin, this chamber was « one of the most elegant creations of vernacular architecture in the Middle Ages » (Germain Bazin, op. cit.) and was the forerunner of the works of Royamont and d'Ourscamp. The Guests' Room is preceded on the south side by the Chapel of St. Made- leine where travellers prayed both before and after meals.

47

THE RAMPARTS
AND THE BUCKLE TOWER
(Tour Boucle)

In the 15th Century, walls were erected right round the town. They were supported by towers, from the north tower with its watchtower (a corbelled stone lookout post overlooking the shorelines) round to the town gates. There are obvious signs of progress when these towers are compared to the old techniques used in the Middle Ages — the system of defence had become all-important in the meantime. The towers are no longer small fortresses built to deal with minor local troubles. Interconnected by a parapet walk as shown in the photograph, they no longer overlook the town walls but on the contrary are defended by them. This is the principle behind modern-day thinking, viz. «whatever provides the defence is itself defended» (Germain Bazin). The ramparts with their numerous projections run close by the houses in the village with machicolations at intervals from which the defending forces could rain projectiles down on the enemy. The Buckle Tower was once known as a small bastion. It juts out over the sand like a spur of rock and its shape is a forerunner of the fortifications built by Vauban. Th[e] horizontal slit windows were mad[e] for bombards, the enormous lar[ge] mediaeval cannon. As a town su[r-] rounded by walls was impregnabl[e,] progress had been made in artiller[y] and in methods of attack. In the di[s-] tance, evening falls over the Breto[n] coast, the marshes around Dol, th[e] polders and the salt-marshes.

Right: The Mont surrounded by th[e] waves, seen from the coast o[f] Avranches.

St.Aubert's spring.

The wars of religion

At the beginning of the 16th. century, one of the King's lieutenants completed the defences of the town. From now on, the entrance to the town was well protected by the Avancée, Boulevard and Roy gates, which were reinforced by the addition of a moat, drawbridge and portcullis.

Throughout the century, the Kings of France visited the famous abbey, and François 1st. was received there with great pomp. But the wars of religion threw the kingdom into confusion, and the Mont was caught up in a whirlwind of battles and massacres.

(continued on page 58)

Right:
BUTTRESSES
ON THE NORTH-EAST
WALL OF THE MARVEL
The «Marvel» is the Gothic section of the abbey. It was built after the destruction of the early 13th Century to replace the Romanesque monastery buildings which had become too small and too uncomfortable. The east wing was the first to be built, and this is the one shown here. It stands on a high bank and comprises three floors symbolising the social hierarchy in the Middle Ages. The poor were given food on the lower floor in the almonry with the groined vaulting reminiscent of traditional Romanesque architecture. On the second floor, the abbot received rich influential visitors in the Guests' Room where

the vaulted ceiling has ribbed arches. Lastly came the refectory, the monks' dining hall, the clergy being deemed to be of prime importance in mediaeval society. Wooden rafters were chosen for this chamber in order to avoid weakening the building. The building overall was supported by mighty buttresses on the outside wall. At refectory level, they were traceried so that they did not block out the light, although in fact they do not jut out far at that particular point. The windows of the great upper chamber are sunk deep into the thick walls. The multilobed arches above them give a somewhat «oriental» appearance to this majestic wall. The battlements along the roof may be an unfortunate piece of 19th-century restoration work.

The Mont seen from the meadows of Brittany.

Overleaf: *The Mont and Tombelaine in the middle of the bay.*

THE CHURCH TOWER

Lightning struck the church tower on numerous occasions, setting fire to the fragile wooden construction. In the Gothic period, a tall spire was flanked by six small pyramidal towers. In the 17th Century, an onion dome was erected and a platform was built onto it in the 18th Century for the benefit of the Chappe telegraph. Finally, the architect Petitgrand designed the present tower. Above its two «Romanesque» storeys is a Gothic spire which is a copy of the one on Notre-Dame Cathedral in Paris. It is topped by a statue of St. Michel bran-dishing his lance as he slays the dragon — a piece of sculpture by Frémiet. And so Mont-Saint-Michel was given its final shape. The lantern-tower flanking the belltower runs all the way up the church from the St. Martin Crypt to the small slate turret. The Maurists once installed a clock in it.

(continued from page 52)

The Protestants tried to capture this Catholic stronghold. Since it was reputed to be impregnable, Captain Le Touchet endeavoured, in 1577, to take it through cunning. Men disguised as pilgrims hid their weapons and managed to get within the walls. They won over the soldiers watching the abbey gates by offering them wine, and then took up their positions on the Saut-Gauthier to await reinforcements. A novice (future monk) from the abbey realised what they were up to and gave the alarm. The monks alerted the townspeople at the foot of the monastery. When they realised they had been discovered, the false pilgrims tried to bluff their way out by shouting "the town has been taken", but the inhabitants took up their arms

to help the monks. Captain Le Touchet, who was just arriving with his horsemen, had to turn back, leaving his companions to surrender.

Another stratagem was used later by members of the formidable Montgomery family. Men disguised as women and fishermen approached the Mont. The guards at the town gate grew suspicious and killed them all in cold blood. The Huguenot troops appeared from nowhere and took the town. But the abbey continued to resist. The military governor was away from the Mont at the time, but as soon as he received news of what was happening, he gathered some men and rushed back. They hoisted themselves up, with the help of ropes, to the ramparts above the

occupied town and started a counter-offensive. The Protestants, caught between two lines of fire, were defeated, and all the prisoners were locked up on Tombelaine Island.

The abbey in ruins

Monastic life was on the wane. The monks began to abandon their abbey : some of them preferred to live in the taverns. They were no longer respected. The abbots, such as Abbot de Guise or Cardinal de Montmorency, were selected by the King from amongst the finest nobility. But they no longer visited the Mont : they were quite content to collect some of its revenue. An unexpected revival took place when new Benedictines, the Maurists, took it over. These learned men

Light rippling across the mudflats.

ere devoted to the history of the
Mont, which they studied from the
collection of manuscripts that had
een built up over the ages.

The buildings were badly maintain-
d and virtually falling into
uin. Both the high towers and
hree supporting arches in the
hurch collapsed. They were not
ebuilt in their original style but
eplaced in 1780 by a very simple
lassical façade.

Meanwhile, the abbey was trans-
ormed into a prison and became
he "sea Bastille". Writs were
ssued by the King to banish to the
sland without fair trial, debauched
ristocrats, corrupt priests and
olitical opponents. The worst of
hem were shut up in dank, dark
lungeons, or, indeed, in Louis XI's
amous cage.

The resurrection of the Mont

The French Revolution got rid
of the last of the monks but the
Mont Saint-Michel continued to be
a prison. From now on, the whole
abbey was a dark and terrible prison. Each riot or failed uprising
brought a new batch of political
prisoners. Victor Hugo evoked
the tragic fate of those men : "All
around us, as far as the eye can
see, infinite space, the blue horizon
of the sea, the green horizon of the
land, clouds, air, liberty, birds
wheeling, ships at full sail ; and
then suddenly, over the top of the
old wall above our heads, the pale
face of a prisoner".

The abbey was rediscovered by
visitors and Romantic writers during
the 19th century. They admired the
extraordinary architecture. This
was the birth of tourism. The prison was abolished under the
Second Empire. In 1874, the
Mont had become a "historic monu-
ment".

The Mont Saint-Michel rose
again from its ruins. Restoration
was undertaken, with extreme
attention to detail. The Gothic
steeple was rebuilt, thus giving the
finishing touch to the famous
silhouette rising above the sand. A
single monk, and then a little community, came and revived the religious tradition. This abbey, which
is also a citadel, bears witness to
one thousand years of effort to
please God, monks and pilgrims
alike.

Sections taken from
« Nous avons bâti
le Mont Saint-Michel »,
Gérard Guillier,
éditions Ouest-France

monks' dorter

monks' gallery

abbey
church

Cyclopean
wall-8th Century

OUR-LADY-UNDERGROUND
Pre-Romanesque church-10th Century

aquilon

Romanesque
almonry
reception room
for the poor

access to
the abbey church

entrance to the
Romanesque abbey

to the church
the hostelry,
the administrative area

THE TRIFORIUM
IN THE CHANCEL
(EARLY 16th CENTURY)

This is the one feature that gives the chancel its architectural and decorative originality. It has ceased to be a horizontal progression round the entire building, as in Chartres or Rheims, and has become a vertical element that is a repetition of the clerestory. This gallery, supported by the arches in the ambulatory, skirts the pillars to avoid weakening them. It is an openwork gallery, like the one in Saint-Ouen, and lets in the light. Flamboyant Gothic architecture turned it into a fine piece of stone tracery with a balustrade borne by three-lobed arches and numerous lancet (elongated ogival arches) topped by a frieze. The ogival arches crown the « glass cage », as F. Enaud termed the top of the chancel. They are interconnected by keystones bearing the coats-of-arms of the abbey and Jean Le Veneur and a carving of St.Michael slaying the dragon.

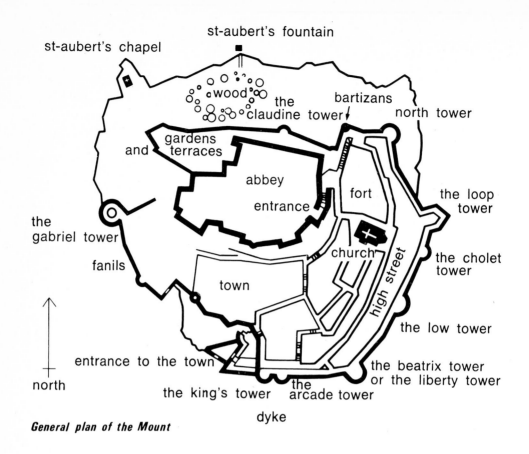

st-aubert's fountain

st-aubert's chapel

wood

the claudine tower

bartizans

north tower

gardens and terraces

abbey entrance

fort

the loop tower

the gabriel tower

church

high street

the cholet tower

fanils

town

the low tower

entrance to the town

the beatrix tower or the liberty tower

north

the king's tower

the arcade tower

dyke

General plan of the Mount

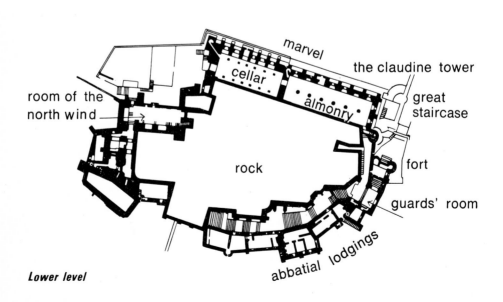

marvel

cellar

the claudine tower

room of the north wind

almonry

great staircase

rock

fort

guards' room

abbatial lodgings

Lower level

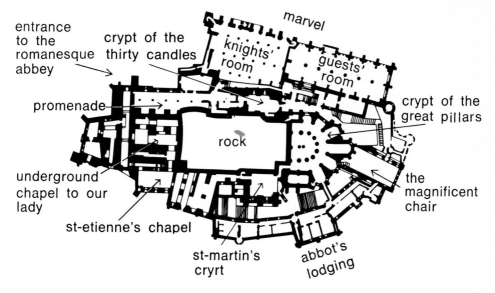

entrance to the romanesque abbey

crypt of the thirty candles

marvel

knights' room

guests' room

promenade

crypt of the great pillars

rock

underground chapel to our lady

the magnificent chair

st-etienne's chapel

st-martin's cryrt

abbot's lodging

Middle level

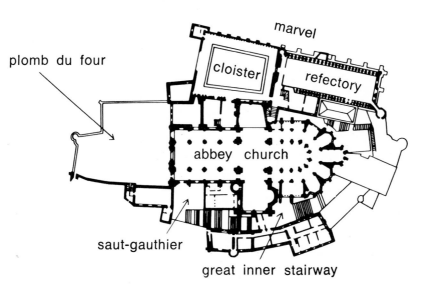

marvel

plomb du four

cloister

refectory

abbey church

saut-gauthier

great inner stairway

Church level

63

PHOTOGRAPHIC CREDITS

Hervé Champollion: Front cover, p. 3, 5, 6, 8-9, 10, 11 (b), 14, 15, 18, 20, 22, 23, 24-25, 26, 27, 30, 31, 33, 36, 44, 50, 54, 56-57, 61, 64, back cover (top).

Jean-Paul Gisserot: p. 2 (t, m, b), 7, 11 (t), 12, 13, 16-17, 19, 21, 28, 29, 32, 34, 35, 37, 38, 40-41, 42, 43, 45, 46, 47, 48-49, 51, 52, 53, 55, 58-59, back cover (b).

Cet ouvrage a été achevé d'imprimer par Offset Aubin à Poitiers - La photocomposition est de l'Atelier Le Dœuff, à Lorient - La couverture a é imprimée par l'imprimerie Raynard à La Guerche-de-Bretagne et pelliculée par la Société des Pelliculages de l'Ouest à Dreux - Le brochage a é réalisé par Mame à Tours - La mise en pages est du Studio des Éditions Ouest-France à Rennes. Opérateur Marcel Oger - Prix à la parution e France continentale : 36 francs français.

© 1986 OUEST-FRANCE – I.S.B.N. 2.85882.977.2 – Dépôt légal : avril 1986 - N° éditeur 1263.01.09.04.86.